# Handbook of Whales

Editor

**Lita Haggerty**

*Scribbles*

Year of Publication 2018

ISBN : 9789352979813

Book Published by

# Scribbles

*(An Imprint of Alpha Editions)*

email - alphaedis@gmail.com

Produced by: PediaPress GmbH
Limburg an der Lahn
Germany
http://pediapress.com/

# Contents

# Whale

<indicator name="pp-default"> 🔒 </indicator> <indicator name="good-star"> ⊕ </indicator>

| Whales |
|---|
| Whales are not a taxon, they are an informal grouping of the infraorder Cetacea |
| |
| Southern right whale |
| **Information** |

| | |
|---|---|
| **Classi-fication of Cetacea** | • Kingdom: Animalia<br>• Phylum: Chordata<br>• Class: Mammalia<br>• Order: Cetartiodactyla<br>• *Clade*: Cetancodontamorpha<br>• Suborder: Whippomorpha<br>• Infraorder: Cetacea |
| **Families consid-ered whales** | • Parvorder Mysticeti<br>  • Family Balaenidae<br>  • Family Balaenopteridae<br>  • Family Eschrichtiidae<br>  • Family Cetotheriidae<br>• Parvorder Odontoceti (excluding dolphins and porpoises)<br>  • Family Monodontidae<br>  • Family Physeteridae<br>  • Family Kogiidae<br>  • Family Ziphiidae |
| • v<br>• t<br>• e[1] | |

**Whales** are a widely distributed and diverse group of fully aquatic placental marine mammals. They are an informal grouping within the infraorder Cetacea, usually excluding dolphins and porpoises. Whales, dolphins and porpoises belong to the order Cetartiodactyla with even-toed ungulates and their closest living relatives are the hippopotamuses, having diverged about 40 million years ago. The two parvorders of whales, baleen whales (Mysticeti) and toothed whales (Odontoceti), are thought to have split apart around 34 million years ago. The whales comprise eight extant families: Balaenopteridae (the rorquals), Balaenidae (right whales), Cetotheriidae (the pygmy right whale), Eschrichtiidae (the grey whale), Monodontidae (belugas and narwhals), Physeteridae (the sperm whale), Kogiidae (the dwarf and pygmy sperm whale), and Ziphiidae (the beaked whales).

Whales are creatures of the open ocean; they feed, mate, give birth, suckle and raise their young at sea. So extreme is their adaptation to life underwater that they are unable to survive on land. Whales range in size from the 2.6 metres (8.5 ft) and 135 kilograms (298 lb) dwarf sperm whale to the 29.9 metres (98 ft) and 190 metric tons (210 short tons) blue whale, which is the largest creature that has ever lived. The sperm whale is the largest toothed predator on earth. Several species exhibit sexual dimorphism, in that the females are larger than males. Baleen whales have no teeth; instead they have plates of baleen, a fringe-like structure used to expel water while retaining the krill and plankton which they feed on. They use their throat pleats to expand the mouth to take in huge gulps of water. Balaenids have heads that can make up 40% of their body mass to take in water. Toothed whales, on the other hand, have conical teeth adapted to catching fish or squid. Baleen whales have a well developed sense of "smell", whereas toothed whales have well-developed hearing – their hearing, that is adapted for both air and water, is so well developed that some can survive even if they are blind. Some species, such as sperm whales, are well adapted for diving to great depths to catch squid and other favoured prey.

Whales have evolved from land-living mammals. As such whales must breathe air regularly, although they can remain submerged under water for long periods of time. Some species such as the sperm whale are able to stay submerged for as much as 90 minutes. They have blowholes (modified nostrils) located on top of their heads, through which air is taken in and expelled. They are warm-blooded, and have a layer of fat, or blubber, under the skin. With streamlined fusiform bodies and two limbs that are modified into flippers, whales can travel at up to 20 knots, though they are not as flexible or agile as seals. Whales produce a great variety of vocalizations, notably the extended songs of the humpback whale. Although whales are widespread, most species prefer the colder waters of the Northern and Southern Hemispheres, and migrate to the equator to give birth. Species such as humpbacks and blue whales are capable of travelling thousands of miles without feeding. Males typically mate with multiple females every year, but females only mate every two to three years. Calves are typically born in the spring and summer months and females bear all the responsibility for raising them. Mothers of some species fast and nurse their young for one to two years.

Once relentlessly hunted for their products, whales are now protected by international law. The North Atlantic right whales nearly became extinct in the twentieth century, with a population low of 450, and the North Pacific grey whale population is ranked Critically Endangered by the IUCN. Besides whaling, they also face threats from bycatch and marine pollution. The meat, blubber and baleen of whales have traditionally been used by indigenous peoples of the Arctic. Whales have been depicted in various cultures worldwide, notably by the Inuit and the coastal peoples of Vietnam and Ghana, who sometimes hold whale funerals. Whales occasionally feature in literature and film, as in the great white whale of Herman Melville's *Moby Dick*. Small whales, such as belugas, are sometimes kept in captivity and trained to perform tricks, but breeding success has been poor and the animals often die within a few months of capture. Whale watching has become a form of tourism around the world.

# Etymology and definitions

The word "whale" comes from the Old English *whæl*, from Proto-Germanic *\*hwalaz*, from Proto Indo European *\*(s)kwal-o-*, meaning "large sea fish". The Proto-Germanic *\*hwalaz* is also the source of Old Saxon *hwal*, Old Norse *hvalr, hvalfiskr*, Swedish *val*, Middle Dutch *wal, walvisc*, Dutch *walvis*, Old High German *wal*, and German *Wal*. The obsolete "whalefish" has a similar derivation, indicating a time when whales were thought to be fish. Wikipedia:Citation needed Other archaic English forms include *wal, wale, whal, whalle, whaille, wheal*, etc.[2]

The term "whale" is sometimes used interchangeably with dolphins and porpoises, acting as a synonym for Cetacea. Six species of dolphins have the word "whale" in their name, collectively known as blackfish: the killer whale, the melon-headed whale, the pygmy killer whale, the false killer whale, and the two species of pilot whales, all of which are classified under the family Delphinidae (oceanic dolphins).[3] Each species has a different reason for it, for example, the killer whale was named "Ballena asesina" by Spanish sailors, which translates directly to "whale assassin" or "whale killer", but is more often translated to "killer whale".

The term "Great Whales" covers those currently regulated by the International Whaling Commission: the Odontoceti family Physeteridae (sperm whales); and the Mysticeti families Balaenidae (right and bowhead whales), Eschrichtiidae (grey whales), and some of the Balaenopteridae (Minke, Bryde's, Sei, Blue and Fin; not Eden's and Omura's whales).

# Taxonomy and evolution

## Phylogeny

The whales are part of the largely terrestrial mammalian clade Laurasiatheria. Whales do not form a clade or order; the infraorder Cetacea includes dolphins and porpoises, which are not considered whales. The phylogenetic tree shows the relationships of whales and other mammals, with whale groups marked in green.

<templatestyles src="Clade/styles.css"></templatestyles>

Laurasiatheriac. 99 mya

<templatestyles src="Clade/styles.css"></templatestyles>

Ferae        (carnivores
             and allies)

Perisso-     (horses,
dactyla      rhinos, tapirs)

Artio-       <templat-
dactyla      estyles
             src="Clade/-
             styles.css"></-
             templatestyles>

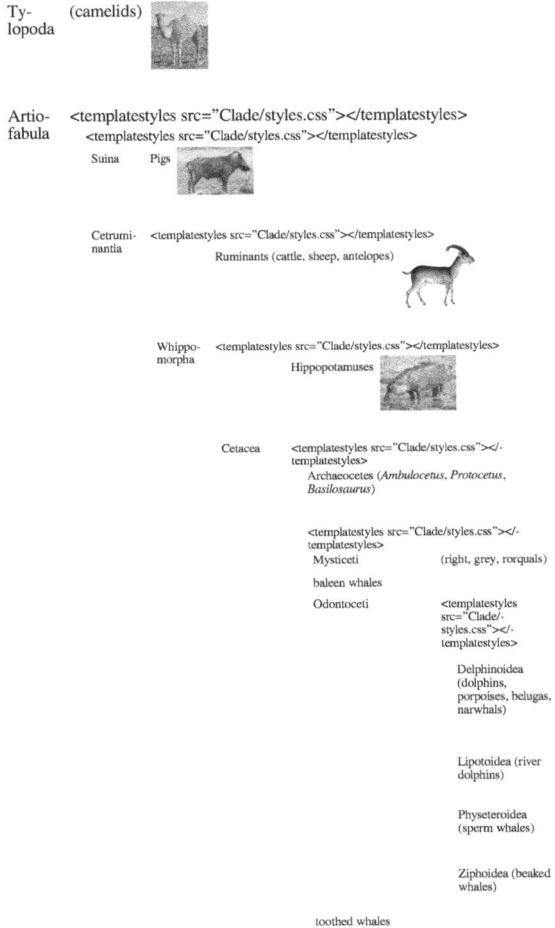

Ty-
lopoda
(camelids)

Artio-
fabula
<templatestyles src="Clade/styles.css"></templatestyles>
<templatestyles src="Clade/styles.css"></templatestyles>

Suina
Pigs

Cetrumi-
nantia
<templatestyles src="Clade/styles.css"></templatestyles>
Ruminants (cattle, sheep, antelopes)

Whippo-
morpha
<templatestyles src="Clade/styles.css"></templatestyles>
Hippopotamuses

Cetacea
<templatestyles src="Clade/styles.css"></-templatestyles>
Archaeocetes (*Ambulocetus, Protocetus, Basilosaurus*)

<templatestyles src="Clade/styles.css"></-templatestyles>
Mysticeti
(right, grey, rorquals)

baleen whales

Odontoceti
<templatestyles src="Clade/styles.css"></-templatestyles>

Delphinoidea (dolphins, porpoises, belugas, narwhals)

Lipotoidea (river dolphins)

Physeteroidea (sperm whales)

Ziphoidea (beaked whales)

toothed whales

c. 53 mya

Cetaceans are divided into two parvorders: the largest parvorder, Mysticeti (baleen whales), is characterized by the presence of baleen, a sieve-like structure in the upper jaw made of keratin, which it uses to filter plankton, among others, from the water; Odontocetes (toothed whales) are characterized by bearing sharp teeth for hunting, as opposed to their counterparts' baleen.[4]

Cetaceans and artiodactyls now are classified under the order Cetartiodactyla, often still referred to as Artiodactyla, which includes both whales and hippopotamuses. The hippopotamus and pygmy hippopotamus are the whale's closest terrestrial living relatives.[5]

## Mysticetes

Mysticetes are also known as baleen whales. They have a pair of blowholes side-by-side and lack teeth; instead they have baleen plates which form a sieve-like structure in the upper jaw made of keratin, which they use to filter plankton from the water. Some whales, such as the humpback, reside in the polar regions where they feed on a reliable source of schooling fish and krill.[6] These animals rely on their well-developed flippers and tail fin to propel themselves through the water; they swim by moving their fore-flippers and tail fin up and down. Whale ribs loosely articulate with their thoracic vertebrae at the proximal end, but do not form a rigid rib cage. This adaptation allows the chest to compress during deep dives as the pressure increases.[7] Mysticetes consist of four families: rorquals (balaenopterids), cetotheriids, right whales (balaenids), and grey whales (eschrichtiids).

The main difference between each family of mysticete is in their feeding adaptations and subsequent behaviour. Balaenopterids are the rorquals. These animals, along with the cetotheriids, rely on their throat pleats to gulp large amounts of water while feeding. The throat pleats extend from the mouth to the navel and allow the mouth to expand to a large volume for more efficient capture of the small animals they feed on. Balaenopterids consist of two genera and eight species.[8] Balaenids are the right whales. These animals have very large heads, which can make up as much as 40% of their body mass, and much of the head is the mouth. This allows them to take in large amounts of water into their mouths, letting them feed more effectively.[9] Eschrichtiids have one living member: the grey whale. They are bottom feeders, mainly eating crustaceans and benthic invertebrates. They feed by turning on their sides and taking in water mixed with sediment, which is then expelled through the baleen, leaving their prey trapped inside. This is an efficient method of hunting, in which the whale has no major competitors.[10]

## Odontocetes

Odontocetes are known as toothed whales; they have teeth and only one blowhole. They rely on their well-developed sonar to find their way in the water. Toothed whales send out ultrasonic clicks using the melon. Sound waves travel through the water. Upon striking an object in the water, the sound waves bounce back at the whale. These vibrations are received through fatty tissues in the jaw, which is then rerouted into the ear-bone and into the brain where the vibrations are interpreted.[11] All toothed whales are opportunistic, meaning they will eat anything they can fit in their throat because they are unable to chew. These animals rely on their well-developed flippers and tail fin to propel themselves through the water; they swim by moving their fore-flippers and tail fin up and down. Whale ribs loosely articulate with their thoracic vertebrae at the proximal end, but they do not form a rigid rib cage. This adaptation allows the chest to compress during deep dives as opposed to resisting the force of water pressure.[7] Excluding dolphins and porpoises, odontocetes consist of four families: belugas and narwhals (monodontids), sperm whales (physeterids), dwarf and pygmy sperm whales (kogiids), and beaked whales (ziphiids). There are six species, sometimes referred to as "blackfish", that are dolphins commonly misconceived as whales: the killer whale, the melon-headed whale, the pygmy killer whale, the false killer whale, and the two species of pilot whales, all of which are classified under the family Delphinidae (oceanic dolphins).[3]

The differences between families of odontocetes include size, feeding adaptations and distribution. Monodontids consist of two species: the beluga and the narwhal. They both reside in the frigid arctic and both have large amounts of blubber. Belugas, being white, hunt in large pods near the surface and around pack ice, their coloration acting as camouflage. Narwhals, being black, hunt in large pods in the aphotic zone, but their underbelly still remains white to remain camouflaged when something is looking directly up or down at them. They have no dorsal fin to prevent collision with pack ice.[12] Physeterids and Kogiids consist of sperm whales. Sperm whales consist the largest and smallest odontocetes, and spend a large portion of their life hunting squid. *P. macrocephalus* spends most of its life in search of squid in the depths; these animals do not require any degree of light at all, in fact, blind sperm whales have been caught in perfect health. The behaviour of Kogiids remains largely unknown, but, due to their small lungs, they are thought to hunt in the photic zone.[13] Ziphiids consist of 22 species of beaked whale. These vary from size, to coloration, to distribution, but they all share a similar hunting style. They use a suction technique, aided by a pair of grooves on the underside of their head, not unlike the throat pleats on the rorquals, to feed.[14]

## Evolution

Whales are descendants of land-dwelling mammals of the artiodactyl order (even-toed ungulates). They are related to the *Indohyus*, an extinct chevrotain-like ungulate, from which they split approximately 48 million years ago.[15,16] Primitive cetaceans, or archaeocetes, first took to the sea approximately 49 million years ago and became fully aquatic 5–10 million years later. What defines an archaeocete is the presence of anatomical features exclusive to cetaceans, alongside other primitive features not found in modern cetaceans, such as visible legs or asymmetrical teeth.[17,18,19,5] Their features became adapted for living in the marine environment. Major anatomical changes included their hearing set-up that channeled vibrations from the jaw to the earbone (*Ambulocetus*

**Figure 1:** *Basilosaurus skeleton*

49 mya), a streamlined body and the growth of flukes on the tail (*Protocetus* 43 mya), the migration of the nostrils toward the top of the cranium (blowholes), and the modification of the forelimbs into flippers (*Basilosaurus* 35 mya), and the shrinking and eventual disappearance of the hind limbs (the first odontocetes and mysticetes 34 mya).[20,21,22]

Whale morphology shows a number of examples of convergent evolution, the most obvious being the streamlined fish-like body shape. Other examples include the use of echolocation for hunting in low light conditions — which is the same hearing adaptation used by bats — and, in the rorqual whales, jaw adaptations, similar to those found in pelicans, that enable engulfment feeding.

Today, the closest living relatives of cetaceans are the hippopotamuses; these share a semi-aquatic ancestor that branched off from other artiodactyls some 60 mya.[5] Around 40 mya, a common ancestor between the two branched off into cetacea and anthracotheres; nearly all anthracotheres became extinct at the end of the Pleistocene 2.5 mya, eventually leaving only one surviving lineage – the hippopotamus.[23]

Whales split into two separate parvorders around 34 mya – the baleen whales (Mysticetes) and the toothed whales (Odontocetes).[24,25,26]

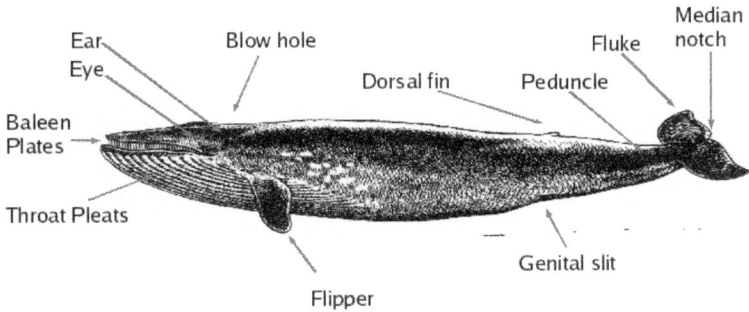

**Figure 2:** *Features of a blue whale*

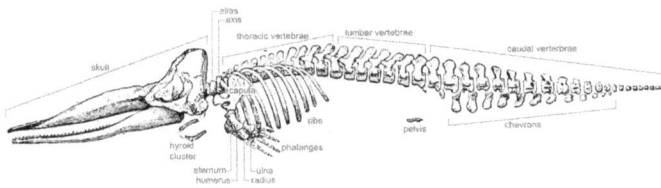

**Figure 3:** *Features of a sperm whale skeleton*

# Biology

## Anatomy

Whales have torpedo shaped bodies with non-flexible necks, limbs modified into flippers, non-existent external ear flaps, a large tail fin, and flat heads (with the exception of monodontids and ziphiids). Whale skulls have small eye orbits, long snouts (with the exception of monodontids and ziphiids) and eyes placed on the sides of its head. Whales range in size from the 2.6-metre (8.5 ft) and 135-kilogram (298 lb) dwarf sperm whale to the 34-metre (112 ft) and 190-metric-ton (210-short-ton) blue whale. Overall, they tend to dwarf other cetartiodactyls; the blue whale is the largest creature on earth. Several species have female-biased sexual dimorphism, with the females being larger than the males. One exception is with the sperm whale, which has males larger than the females.[27,28]

Odontocetes, such as the sperm whale, possess teeth with cementum cells overlying dentine cells. Unlike human teeth, which are composed mostly of enamel on the portion of the tooth outside of the gum, whale teeth have cementum outside the gum. Only in larger whales, where the cementum is worn away on

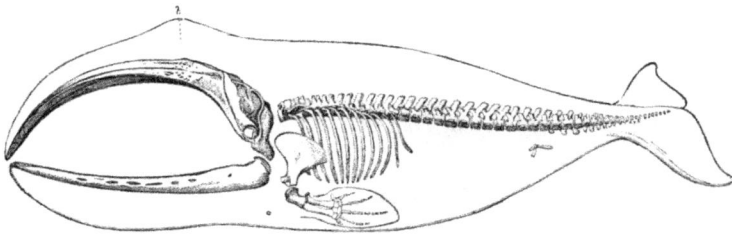

**Figure 4:** *Skeleton of a bowhead whale; notice the hind limb. Richard Lydekker, 1894*

the tip of the tooth, does enamel show. Mysticetes have large whalebone, as opposed to teeth, made of keratin. Mysticetes have two blowholes, whereas Odontocetes contain only one.[29]

Breathing involves expelling stale air from the blowhole, forming an upward, steamy spout, followed by inhaling fresh air into the lungs; a humpback whale's lungs can hold about 5,000 litres of air. Spout shapes differ among species, which facilitates identification.[30,31]

The heart of a whale weighs about 180–200 kg. It is 640 times bigger than a human heart. The heart of the blue whale is the largest of any animal, and the walls of the arteries in the heart have been described as being "as thick as an iPhone 6 Plus is long".

All whales have a thick layer of blubber. In species that live near the poles, the blubber can be as thick as 11 inches. This blubber can help with buoyancy (which is helpful for a 100-ton whale), protection to some extent as predators would have a hard time getting through a thick layer of fat, and energy for fasting when migrating to the equator; the primary usage for blubber is insulation from the harsh climate. It can constitute as much as 50% of a whale's body weight. Calves are born with only a thin layer of blubber, but some species compensate for this with thick lanugos.[32,33]

Whales have a two- to three-chambered stomach that is similar in structure to terrestrial carnivores. Mysticetes contain a proventriculus as an extension of the oesophagus; this contains stones that grind up food. They also have fundic and pyloric chambers.[34]

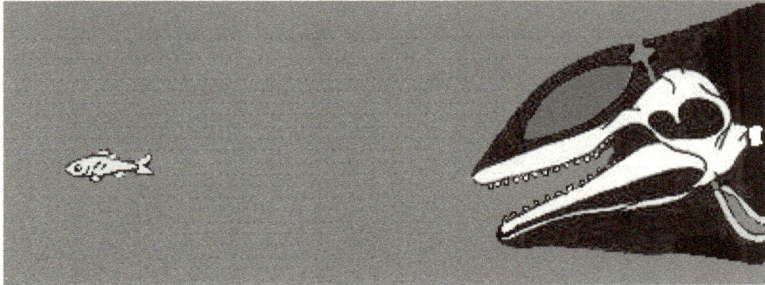

**Figure 5:** *Biosonar by cetaceans*

## Locomotion

Whales have two flippers on the front, and a tail fin. These flippers contain four digits. Although whales do not possess fully developed hind limbs, some, such as the sperm whale and bowhead whale, possess discrete rudimentary appendages, which may contain feet and digits. Whales are fast swimmers in comparison to seals, which typically cruise at 5–15 kn, or 9–28 kilometres per hour (5.6–17.4 mph); the fin whale, in comparison, can travel at speeds up to 47 kilometres per hour (29 mph) and the sperm whale can reach speeds of 35 kilometres per hour (22 mph). The fusing of the neck vertebrae, while increasing stability when swimming at high speeds, decreases flexibility; whales are unable to turn their heads. When swimming, whales rely on their tail fin propel them through the water. Flipper movement is continuous. Whales swim by moving their tail fin and lower body up and down, propelling themselves through vertical movement, while their flippers are mainly used for steering. Some species log out of the water, which may allow them to travel faster. Their skeletal anatomy allows them to be fast swimmers. Most species have a dorsal fin.[35,36]

Whales are adapted for diving to great depths. In addition to their streamlined bodies, they can slow their heart rate to conserve oxygen; blood is rerouted from tissue tolerant of water pressure to the heart and brain among other organs; haemoglobin and myoglobin store oxygen in body tissue; and they have twice the concentration of myoglobin than haemoglobin. Before going on long dives, many whales exhibit a behaviour known as sounding; they stay close to the surface for a series of short, shallow dives while building their oxygen reserves, and then make a sounding dive.[7,37]

## Senses

The whale ear has specific adaptations to the marine environment. In humans, the middle ear works as an impedance equalizer between the outside

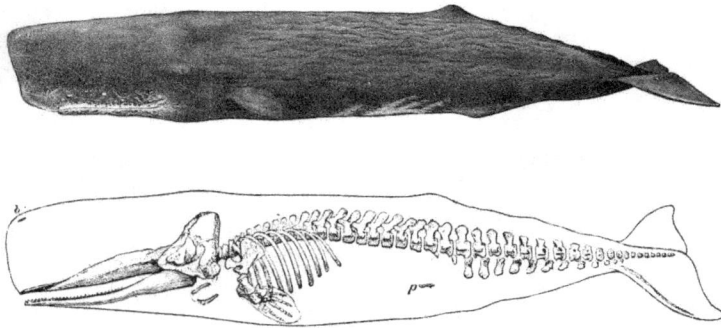

**Figure 6:** *Sperm whale skeleton. Richard Lydekker, 1894.*

air's low impedance and the cochlear fluid's high impedance. In whales, and other marine mammals, there is no great difference between the outer and inner environments. Instead of sound passing through the outer ear to the middle ear, whales receive sound through the throat, from which it passes through a low-impedance fat-filled cavity to the inner ear.[38] The whale ear is acoustically isolated from the skull by air-filled sinus pockets, which allow for greater directional hearing underwater.[39] Odontocetes send out high frequency clicks from an organ known as a melon. This melon consists of fat, and the skull of any such creature containing a melon will have a large depression. The melon size varies between species, the bigger the more dependent they are of it. A beaked whale for example has a small bulge sitting on top of its skull, whereas a sperm whale's head is filled up mainly with the melon.[40,41,42,43]

The whale eye is relatively small for its size, yet they do retain a good degree of eyesight. As well as this, the eyes of a whale are placed on the sides of its head, so their vision consists of two fields, rather than a binocular view like humans have. When belugas surface, their lens and cornea correct the nearsightedness that results from the refraction of light; they contain both rod and cone cells, meaning they can see in both dim and bright light, but they have far more rod cells than they do cone cells. Whales do, however, lack short wavelength sensitive visual pigments in their cone cells indicating a more limited capacity for colour vision than most mammals.[44] Most whales have slightly flattened eyeballs, enlarged pupils (which shrink as they surface to prevent damage), slightly flattened corneas and a tapetum lucidum; these adaptations allow for large amounts of light to pass through the eye and, therefore, a very clear image of the surrounding area. They also have glands on the eyelids and outer corneal layer that act as protection for the cornea.[45,46]

The olfactory lobes are absent in toothed whales, suggesting that they have no sense of smell. Some whales, such as the bowhead whale, possess a vomeronasal organ, which does mean that they can "sniff out" krill.[47]

Whales are not thought to have a good sense of taste, as their taste buds are atrophied or missing altogether. However, some toothed whales have preferences between different kinds of fish, indicating some sort of attachment to taste. The presence of the Jacobson's organ indicates that whales can smell food once inside their mouth, which might be similar to the sensation of taste.[48]

## Communication

Humpback whale "song"
Recording of Humpback Whales singing and Clicking.

*Problems playing this file? See media help.*

Whale vocalization is likely to serve several purposes. Some species, such as the humpback whale, communicate using melodic sounds, known as whale song. These sounds may be extremely loud, depending on the species. Humpback whales only have been heard making clicks, while toothed whales use sonar that may generate up to 20,000 watts of sound (+73 dBm or +43 dBw)[49] and be heard for many miles.

Captive whales have occasionally been known to mimic human speech. Scientists have suggested this indicates a strong desire on behalf of the whales to communicate with humans, as whales have a very different vocal mechanism, so imitating human speech likely takes considerable effort.[50]

Whales emit two distinct kinds of acoustic signals, which are called whistles and clicks:[51] Clicks are quick broadband burst pulses, used for sonar, although some lower-frequency broadband vocalizations may serve a non-echolocative purpose such as communication; for example, the pulsed calls of belugas. Pulses in a click train are emitted at intervals of $\sim$35–50 milliseconds, and in general these inter-click intervals are slightly greater than the round-trip time of sound to the target. Whistles are narrow-band frequency modulated (FM) signals, used for communicative purposes, such as contact calls.

**Figure 7:** *Bubble net feeding*

## Intelligence

Whales are known to teach, learn, cooperate, scheme, and grieve.[52] The neo-cortex of many species of whale is home to elongated spindle neurons that, prior to 2007, were known only in hominids.[53] In humans, these cells are involved in social conduct, emotions, judgement, and theory of mind. Whale spindle neurons are found in areas of the brain that are homologous to where they are found in humans, suggesting that they perform a similar function.[54]

Brain size was previously considered a major indicator of the intelligence of an animal. Since most of the brain is used for maintaining bodily functions, greater ratios of brain to body mass may increase the amount of brain mass available for more complex cognitive tasks. Allometric analysis indicates that mammalian brain size scales at approximately the ⅔ or ¾ exponent of the body mass. Comparison of a particular animal's brain size with the expected brain size based on such allometric analysis provides an encephalisation quotient that can be used as another indication of animal intelligence. Sperm whales have the largest brain mass of any animal on earth, averaging 8,000 cubic centimetres (490 in³) and 7.8 kilograms (17 lb) in mature males, in comparison to the average human brain which averages 1,450 cubic centimetres (88 in³) in mature males.[55] The brain to body mass ratio in some odontocetes, such as belugas and narwhals, is second only to humans.[56]

Small whales are known to engage in complex play behaviour, which includes such things as producing stable underwater toroidal air-core vortex rings or

**Figure 8:** *A southern right whale sailing*

"bubble rings". There are two main methods of bubble ring production: rapid puffing of a burst of air into the water and allowing it to rise to the surface, forming a ring, or swimming repeatedly in a circle and then stopping to inject air into the helical vortex currents thus formed. They also appear to enjoy biting the vortex-rings, so that they burst into many separate bubbles and then rise quickly to the surface.[57] Some believe this is a means of communication.[58] Whales are also known to produce bubble-nets for the purpose of foraging.[59]

Larger whales are also thought, to some degree, to engage in play. The southern right whale, for example, elevates their tail fluke above the water, remaining in the same position for a considerable amount of time. This is known as "sailing". It appears to be a form of play and is most commonly seen off the coast of Argentina and South Africa. Humpback whales, among others, are also known to display this behaviour.[60]

## Life cycle

Whales are fully aquatic creatures, which means that birth and courtship behaviours are very different from terrestrial and semi-aquatic creatures. Since they are unable to go onto land to calve, they deliver the baby with the fetus positioned for tail-first delivery. This prevents the baby from drowning either upon or during delivery. To feed the new-born, whales, being aquatic, must squirt the milk into the mouth of the calf. Being mammals, they have mammary glands used for nursing calves; they are weaned off at about 11 months of age. This milk contains high amounts of fat which is meant to hasten the development of blubber; it contains so much fat that it has the consistency of toothpaste.[61] Females deliver a single calf with gestation lasting about a year, dependency until one to two years, and maturity around seven to ten years, all varying between the species.[62] This mode of reproduction produces few offspring, but increases the survival probability of each one. Females, referred to as "cows", carry the responsibility of childcare as males, referred to as "bulls", play no part in raising calves.

Most mysticetes reside at the poles. So, to prevent the unborn calf from dying of frostbite, they migrate to calving/mating grounds. They will then stay there for a matter of months until the calf has developed enough blubber to survive the bitter temperatures of the poles. Until then, the calves will feed on the mother's fatty milk.[63] With the exception of the humpback whale, it is largely unknown when whales migrate. Most will travel from the Arctic or Antarctic into the tropics to mate, calve, and raise during the winter and spring; they will migrate back to the poles in the warmer summer months so the calf can continue growing while the mother can continue eating, as they fast in the breeding grounds. One exception to this is the southern right whale, which migrates to Patagonia and western New Zealand to calve; both are well out of the tropic zone.[64]

## Sleep

Unlike most animals, whales are conscious breathers. All mammals sleep, but whales cannot afford to become unconscious for long because they may drown. While knowledge of sleep in wild cetaceans is limited, toothed cetaceans in captivity have been recorded to sleep with one side of their brain at a time, so that they may swim, breathe consciously, and avoid both predators and social contact during their period of rest.[65]

A 2008 study found that sperm whales sleep in vertical postures just under the surface in passive shallow 'drift-dives', generally during the day, during which whales do not respond to passing vessels unless they are in contact, leading to the suggestion that whales possibly sleep during such dives.[65]

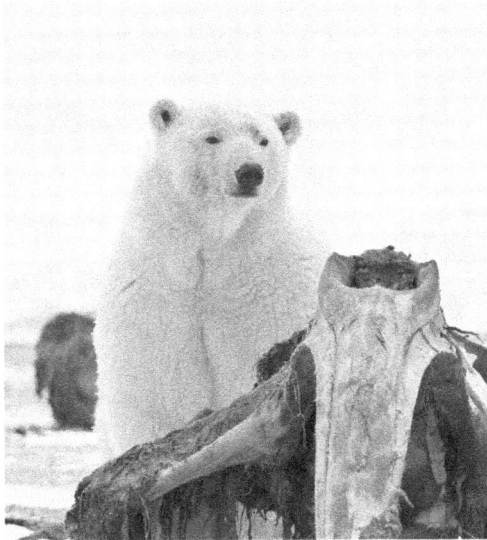

**Figure 9:** *Polar bear with the remains of a beluga*

# Ecology

## Foraging and predation

All whales are carnivorous and predatory. Odontocetes, as a whole, mostly feed on fish and cephalopods, and then followed by crustaceans and bivalves. All species are generalist and opportunistic feeders. Mysticetes, as a whole, mostly feed on krill and plankton, followed by crustaceans and other invertebrates. A few are specialists. Examples include the blue whale, which eats almost exclusively krill, the minke whale, which eats mainly schooling fish, the sperm whale, which specialize on squid, and the grey whale which feed on bottom-dwelling invertebrates.[8,66,67] The elaborate baleen "teeth" of filter-feeding species, mysticetes, allow them to remove water before they swallow their planktonic food by using the teeth as a sieve.[61] Usually whales hunt solitarily, but they do sometimes hunt cooperatively in small groups. The former behaviour is typical when hunting non-schooling fish, slow-moving or immobile invertebrates or endothermic prey. When large amounts of prey are available, whales such as certain mysticetes hunt cooperatively in small groups.[68] Some cetaceans may forage with other kinds of animals, such as other species of whales or certain species of pinnipeds.[69,70]

Large whales, such as mysticetes, are not usually subject to predation, but smaller whales, such as monodontids or ziphiids, are. These species are preyed

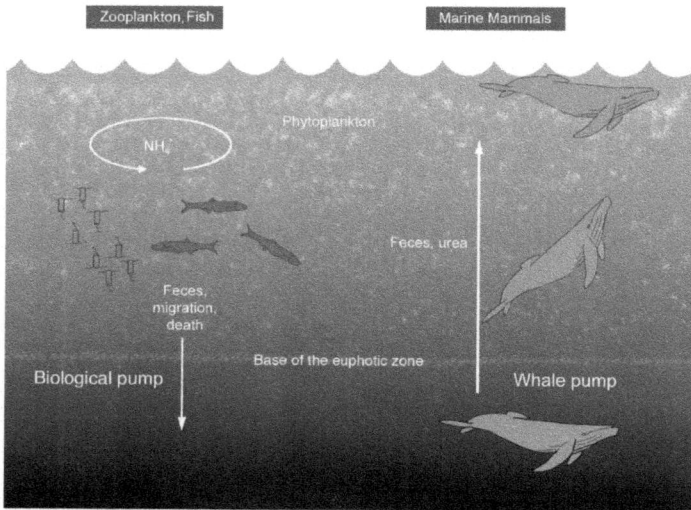

**Figure 10:** *"Whale pump" – the role played*
*by whales in recycling ocean nutrients*[73]

on by the killer whale or orca. To subdue and kill whales, orcas continuously ram them with their heads; this can sometimes kill bowhead whales, or severely injure them. Other times they corral the narwhals or belugas before striking. They are typically hunted by groups of 10 or fewer orcas, but they are seldom attacked by an individual. Calves are more commonly taken by orcas, but adults can be targeted as well.[71]

These small whales are also targeted by terrestrial and pagophilic predators. The polar bear is well adapted for hunting Arctic whales and calves. Bears are known to use sit-and-wait tactics as well as active stalking and pursuit of prey on ice or water. Whales lessen the chance of predation by gathering in groups. This however means less room around the breathing hole as the ice slowly closes the gap. When out at sea, whales dive out of the reach of surface-hunting orcas. Polar bear attacks on belugas and narwhals are usually successful in winter, but rarely inflict any damage in summer.[72]

## Whale pump

A 2010 study considered whales to be a positive influence to the productivity of ocean fisheries, in what has been termed a "whale pump." Whales carry nutrients such as nitrogen from the depths back to the surface. This functions as an upward biological pump, reversing an earlier presumption that whales accelerate the loss of nutrients to the bottom. This nitrogen input in the Gulf of Maine is "more than the input of all rivers combined" emptying into the gulf, some 23,000 metric tons (25,000 short tons) each year.[74,75] Whales defecate at the ocean's surface; their excrement is important for fisheries because it is rich in iron and nitrogen. The whale faeces are liquid and instead of sinking, they stay at the surface where phytoplankton feed off it.[75,76,77]

## Whale fall

Upon death, whale carcasses fall to the deep ocean and provide a substantial habitat for marine life. Evidence of whale falls in present-day and fossil records shows that deep sea whale falls support a rich assemblage of creatures, with a global diversity of 407 species, comparable to other neritic biodiversity hotspots, such as cold seeps and hydrothermal vents.[78]

Deterioration of whale carcasses happens though a series of three stages. Initially, moving organisms such as sharks and hagfish, scavenge the soft tissues at a rapid rate over a period of months, and as long as two years. This is followed by the colonization of bones and surrounding sediments (which contain organic matter) by enrichment opportunists, such as crustaceans and polychaetes, throughout a period of years. Finally, sulfophilic bacteria reduce the bones releasing hydrogen sulfide enabling the growth of chemoautotrophic organisms, which in turn, support other organisms such as mussels, clams, limpets, and sea snails. This stage may last for decades and supports a rich assemblage of species, averaging 185 species per site.[78,79]

# Interaction with humans

## Whaling

Whaling by humans has existed since the Stone Age. Ancient whalers used harpoons to spear the bigger animals from boats out at sea.[80] People from Norway and Japan started hunting whales around 2000 B.C.[81] Whales are typically hunted for their meat and blubber by aboriginal groups; they used baleen for baskets or roofing, and made tools and masks out of bones.[81] The Inuit hunted whales in the Arctic Ocean.[81] The Basques started whaling as early as the 11th century, sailing as far as Newfoundland in the 16th century in search of right whales.[82,83] 18th- and 19th-century whalers hunted whales mainly for their oil, which was used as lamp fuel and a lubricant, baleen or whalebone, which was used for items such as corsets and skirt hoops,[81] and ambergris, which was used as a fixative for perfumes. The most successful whaling nations at this time were the Netherlands, Japan, and the United States.[84]

Fig. 194.—Whale-Fishing.—Fac-simile of a Woodcut in the "Cosmographie Universelle" or
Thevet, in folio: Paris, 1574.

**Figure 11:** *Whale Fishing: Woodcut by Thevet, Paris, 1574*

**Figure 12:** *Dutch whalers near Spitsbergen, their
most successful port. Abraham Storck, 1690*

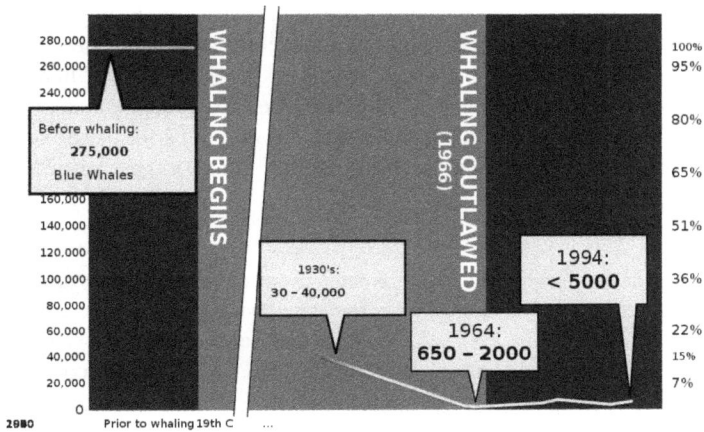

**Figure 13:** *World population graph of blue whales*

Commercial whaling was historically important as an industry well throughout the 17th, 18th and 19th centuries. Whaling was at that time a sizeable European industry with ships from Britain, France, Spain, Denmark, the Netherlands and Germany, sometimes collaborating to hunt whales in the Arctic, sometimes in competition leading even to war.[85] By the early 1790s, whalers, namely the Americans and Australians, focused efforts in the South Pacific where they mainly hunted sperm whales and right whales, with catches of up to 39,000 right whales by Americans alone.[82,86] By 1853, US profits reached US$11,000,000 (UK£6.5m), equivalent to US$348,000,000 (UK£230m) today, the most profitable year for the American whaling industry.[87] Commonly exploited species included North Atlantic right whales, sperm whales, which were mainly hunted by Americans, bowhead whales, which were mainly hunted by the Dutch, common minke whales, blue whales, and grey whales. The scale of whale harvesting decreased substantially after 1982 when the International Whaling Commission (IWC) placed a moratorium which set a catch limit for each country, excluding aboriginal groups until 2004.[88]

Current whaling nations are Norway, Iceland, and Japan, despite their joining to the IWC, as well as the aboriginal communities of Siberia, Alaska, and northern Canada.[89] Subsistence hunters typically use whale products for themselves and depend on them for survival. National and international authorities have given special treatment to aboriginal hunters since their methods of hunting are seen as less destructive and wasteful. This distinction is being questioned as these aboriginal groups are using more modern weaponry and mechanized transport to hunt with, and are selling whale products in the marketplace. Some anthropologists argue that the term "subsistence" should also apply to these cash-based exchanges as long as they take place within local production and consumption.[90,91,92] In 1946, the IWC placed a moratorium, limiting the annual whale catch. Since then, yearly profits for these "subsistence" hunters have been close to US$31 million (UK£20m) per year.[88]

## Other threats

Whales can also be threatened by humans more indirectly. They are unintentionally caught in fishing nets by commercial fisheries as bycatch and accidentally swallow fishing hooks. Gillnetting and Seine netting is a significant cause of mortality in whales and other marine mammals.[93] Species commonly entangled include beaked whales. Whales are also affected by marine pollution. High levels of organic chemicals accumulate in these animals since they are high in the food chain. They have large reserves of blubber, more so for toothed whales as they are higher up the food chain than baleen whales. Lactating mothers can pass the toxins on to their young. These pollutants can cause gastrointestinal cancers and greater vulnerability to infectious diseases.[94] They can also be poisoned by swallowing litter, such as plastic bags.[95] Advanced military sonar harms whales. Sonar interferes with the basic biological functions of whales—such as feeding and mating—by impacting their ability to echolocate. Whales swim in response to sonar and sometimes experience decompression sickness due to rapid changes in depth. Mass strandings have been triggered by sonar activity, resulting in injury or death.[96]

## Conservation

Whaling decreased substantially after 1946 when, in response to the steep decline in whale populations, the International Whaling Commission placed a moratorium which set a catch limit for each country; this excluded aboriginal groups up until 2004.[84,91,97,98] As of 2015, aboriginal communities are allowed to take 280 bowhead whales off Alaska and two from the western coast of Greenland, 620 grey whales off Washington state, three common minke whales off the eastern coast of Greenland and 178 on their western coast, 10 fin whales from the west coast of Greenland, nine humpback whales from the west coast of Greenland and 20 off St. Vincent and the Grenadines each year.[98] Several species that were commercially exploited have rebounded in numbers; for example, grey whales may be as numerous as they were prior to harvesting, but the North Atlantic population is functionally extinct. Conversely, the North Atlantic right whale was extirpated from much of its former range, which stretched across the North Atlantic, and only remains in small fragments along

**Figure 14:** *World map showing International Whaling Commission (IWC) members in blue*

the coast of Canada, Greenland, and is considered functionally extinct along the European coastline.[99]

The IWC has designated two whale sanctuaries: the Southern Ocean Whale Sanctuary, and the Indian Ocean Whale Sanctuary. The Southern Ocean whale sanctuary spans 30,560,860 square kilometres (11,799,610 sq mi) and envelopes Antarctica.[100] The Indian Ocean whale sanctuary takes up all of the Indian Ocean south of 55°S.[101] The IWC is a voluntary organization, with no treaty. Any nation may leave as they wish; the IWC cannot enforce any law it makes.

As of 2013, the International Union for Conservation of Nature (IUCN) recognized 86 cetacean species, 40 of which are considered whales. Six are considered at risk, as they are ranked Critically Endangered (the North Atlantic right whale), "Endangered" (blue whale, fin whale, North Pacific right whale, and sei whale), and "Vulnerable" (sperm whale). Twenty-one species have a "Data Deficient" ranking.[102] Species that live in polar habitats are vulnerable to the effects of recent and ongoing climate change, particularly the time when pack ice forms and melts.[103]

## Whale watching

An estimated 13 million people went whale watching globally in 2008, in all oceans except the Arctic.[104] Rules and codes of conduct have been created to minimize harassment of the whales.[105] Iceland, Japan and Norway have both whaling and whale watching industries. Whale watching lobbyists are concerned that the most inquisitive whales, which approach boats closely and provide much of the entertainment on whale-watching trips, will be the first to be taken if whaling is resumed in the same areas.[106] Whale watching generated

**Figure 15:** *Whale watching off Bar Harbour, Maine*

US$2.1 billion (UK£1.4 billion) per annum in tourism revenue worldwide, employing around 13,000 workers.[107] In contrast, the whaling industry, with the moratorium in place, generates US$31 million (UK£20 million) per year.[88] The size and rapid growth of the industry has led to complex and continuing debates with the whaling industry about the best use of whales as a natural resource.

## In myth, literature and art

As marine creatures that reside in either the depths or the poles, humans knew very little about whales over the course of history; many feared or revered them. The Nords and various arctic tribes revered the whale as they were important pieces of their lives. In Inuit creation myths, when 'Big Raven', a deity in human form, found a stranded whale, he was told by the Great Spirit where to find special mushrooms that would give him the strength to drag the whale back to the sea and thus, return order to the world. In an Icelandic legend, a man threw a stone at a fin whale and hit the blowhole, causing the whale to burst. The man was told not to go to sea for twenty years, but during the nineteenth year he went fishing and a whale came and killed him.

Whales played a major part in shaping the art forms of many coastal civilizations, such as the Norse, with some dating to the Stone Age. Petroglyphs off a

**Figure 16:** *Engraving by William van der Gouwen depicting a stranded sperm whale being butchered on the Dutch coast, 1598*

**Figure 17:** *Whalers off Twofold Bay, New South Wales. Watercolour by Oswald Brierly, 1867*

**Figure 18:** *Illustration by Gustave Doré of Baron Munchausen's tale of being swallowed by a whale. While the Biblical Book of Jonah refers to the Prophet Jonah being swallowed by "a big fish", in later derivations that "fish" was identified as a whale.*

cliff face in Bangudae, South Korea show 300 depictions of various animals, a third of which are whales. Some show particular detail in which there are throat pleats, typical of rorquals. These petroglyphs show these people, of around 7,000 to 3,500 B.C.E. in South Korea, had a very high dependency on whales.[108]

The Pacific Islanders and Australian Aborigines viewed whales as bringers of good and joy. One exception is French Polynesia, where, in many parts, cetaceans are met with great brutality.[109]

In Vietnam and Ghana, among other places, whales hold a sense of divinity. They are so respected in their cultures that they occasionally hold funerals for beached whales, a throwback to Vietnam's ancient sea-based Austro-Asiatic culture.[110,111,112,113] The god of the seas, according to Chinese folklore, was a large whale with human limbs.

Whales have also played a role in sacred texts such as the Bible. It mentions whales in Genesis 1:21, Job 7:12, and Ezekiel 32:2. The "leviathan" described at length in Job 41:1-34 is generally understood to refer to a whale. The "sea monsters" in Lamentations 4:3 have been taken by some to refer to marine mammals, in particular whales, although most modern versions use the word "jackals" instead.[114] The story of Jonah being swallowed by a great fish is told both in the Qur'an and in the Bible. A medieval column capital sculpture depicting this was made in the 12th century in the abbey church in Mozac, France.[115] The Old Testament contains the Book of Jonah and in the New Testament, Jesus mentions this story in Matthew 12:40.[116]

In 1585, Alessandro Farnese, 1585, and Francois, Duke of Anjou, 1582, were greeted on his ceremonial entry into the port city of Antwerp by floats including "Neptune and the Whale", indicating at least the city's dependence on the sea for its wealth.[117]

In 1896, an article in *The Pall Mall Gazette* popularised a practice of alternative medicine that probably began in the whaling town of Eden, Australia two or three years earlier. It was believed that climbing inside a whale carcass and remaining there for a few hours would relief symptoms of rheumatism.

Whales continue to be prevalent in modern literature. For example, Herman Melville's *Moby Dick* features a "great white whale" as the main antagonist for Ahab, who eventually is killed by it. The whale is an albino sperm whale, considered by Melville to be the largest type of whale, and is partly based on the historically attested bull whale Mocha Dick. Rudyard Kipling's *Just So Stories* includes the story of "How the Whale got in his Throat". Niki Caro's film the *Whale Rider* has a Māori girl ride a whale in her journey to be a suitable heir to the chieftain-ship. Walt Disney's film *Pinocchio* features a giant whale named Monstro as the final antagonist. Alan Hovhaness' orchestra *And God Created Great Whales* included the recorded sounds of humpback and bowhead whales.[118] Léo Ferré's song "Il n'y a plus rien" is an example of biomusic that begins and ends with recorded whale songs mixed with a symphonic orchestra and his voice.

### In captivity

Belugas were the first whales to be kept in captivity. Other species were too rare, too shy, or too big. The first beluga was shown at Barnum's Museum in New York City in 1861.[119] For most of the 20th century, Canada was the predominant source of wild belugas.[120] They were taken from the St. Lawrence River estuary until the late 1960s, after which they were predominantly taken from the Churchill River estuary until capture was banned in 1992.[120] Russia has become the largest provider since it had been banned in Canada.[120] Belugas are caught in the Amur River delta and their eastern coast, and then are either transported domestically to aquariums or dolphinariums in Moscow, St. Petersburg, and Sochi, or exported to other countries, such as Canada.[120] Most captive belugas are caught in the wild, since captive-breeding programs are not very successful.[121]

**Figure 19:** *Beluga whales and trainers in an aquarium*

As of 2006, 30 belugas were in Canada and 28 in the United States, and 42 deaths in captivity had been reported up to that time.[120] A single specimen can reportedly fetch up to US$100,000 (UK£64,160) on the market. The beluga's popularity is due to its unique colour and its facial expressions. The latter is possible because while most cetacean "smiles" are fixed, the extra movement afforded by the beluga's unfused cervical vertebrae allows a greater range of apparent expression.[122]

Between 1960 and 1992, the Navy carried out a program that included the study of marine mammals' abilities with sonar, with the objective of improving the detection of underwater objects. A large number of belugas were used from 1975 on, the first being dolphins.[122,123] The program also included training them to carry equipment and material to divers working underwater by holding cameras in their mouths to locate lost objects, survey ships and submarines, and underwater monitoring.[123] A similar program was used by the Russian Navy during the Cold War, in which belugas were also trained for antimining operations in the Arctic.[124]

Aquariums have tried housing other species of whales in captivity. The success of belugas turned attention to maintaining their relative, the narwhal, in captivity. However, in repeated attempts in the 1960s and 1970s, all narwhals kept in captivity died within months. A pair of pygmy right whales were retained in an enclosed area (with nets); they were eventually released in South

Africa. There was one attempt to keep a stranded Sowerby's beaked whale calf in captivity; the calf rammed into the tank wall, breaking its rostrum, which resulted in death. It was thought that Sowerby's beaked whale evolved to swim fast in a straight line, and a 30-metre (98 ft) tank was not big enough.[125] There have been attempts to keep baleen whales in captivity. There were three attempts to keep grey whales in captivity. Gigi was a grey whale calf that died in transport. Gigi II was another grey whale calf that was captured in the Ojo de Liebre Lagoon, and was transported to SeaWorld.[126] The 680-kilogram (1,500 lb) calf was a popular attraction, and behaved normally, despite being separated from his mother. A year later, the 8,000-kilogram (18,000 lb) whale grew too big to keep in captivity and was released; it was the first of two grey whales, the other being another grey whale calf named JJ, to successfully be kept in captivity.[126] There were three attempts to keep minke whales in captivity in Japan. They were kept in a tidal pool with a sea-gate at the Izu Mito Sea Paradise. Another, unsuccessful, attempt was made by the U.S.[127] One stranded humpback whale calf was kept in captivity for rehabilitation, but died days later.[128]

# Bibliography

## Books

<templatestyles src="Refbegin/styles.css" />

- Klinowska, Margaret; Cooke, Justin (1991). *Dolphins, Porpoises, and Whales of the World: the IUCN Red Data Book*[129] (PDF). Columbia University Press, NY: IUCN Publications. ISBN 978-2-88032-936-5.<templatestyles src="Module:Citation/CS1/styles.css"></templatestyles>
- Thomas, Jeanette A.; Kastelein, Ronald A. (1990). *Sensory Abilities of Cetaceans: Laboratory and Field Evidence*[130]. **196**. New York: Springer Science & Business Media. doi: 10.1007/978-1-4899-0858-2[131]. ISBN 978-1-4899-0860-5.<templatestyles src="Module:Citation/CS1/styles.css"></templatestyles>
- Leatherwood, S.; Prematunga, W.P.; Girton, P.; McBrearty, D.; Ilangakoon, A.; McDonald, D (1991). Records of 'blackfish' (killer, false killer, pilot, pygmy killer, and melon-headed whales) in the Indian Ocean Sanctuary, 1772-1986 in *Cetaceans and cetacean research in the Indian Ocean Sanctuary*. UNEP Marine Mammal Technical Report. pp. 33–65. ASIN B00KX9I8Y8[132].<templatestyles src="Module:Citation/CS1/styles.css"></templatestyles>

- Skeat, Walter W. (1898). *An Etymological Dictionary of the English Language*[133] (3 ed.). Clarendon Press. p. 704.<templatestyles src="Module:Citation/CS1/styles.css"></templatestyles>
- Dawkins, Richard (2004). *The Ancestor's Tale, A Pilgrimage to the Dawn of Life*. Houghton Mifflin. ISBN 0-618-00583-8.<templatestyles src="Module:Citation/CS1/styles.css"></templatestyles>
- *Shorter Oxford English dictionary*. United Kingdom: Oxford University Press. 2007. p. 3804.<templatestyles src="Module:Citation/CS1/styles.css"></templatestyles>
- Ralls, Katherine; Mesnick, Sarah (1984). "Sexual Dimorphism"[134] (PDF). *Encyclopedia of Marine Mammals* (2nd ed.). San Diego: Academic Press. pp. 1005–1011. ISBN 978-0-08-091993-5.<templatestyles src="Module:Citation/CS1/styles.css"></templatestyles>
- Stevens, C. Edward; Hume, Ian D. (1995). *Comparative Physiology of the Vertebrate Digestive System*[135]. Cambridge University Press. p. 317. ISBN 978-0-521-44418-7.<templatestyles src="Module:Citation/CS1/styles.css"></templatestyles>
- Thewissen, J. G. M.; Perrin, William R.; Wirsig, Bernd (2002). "Hearing". *Encyclopedia of Marine Mammals*. San Diego: Academic Press. pp. 570–572. ISBN 978-0-12-551340-1.<templatestyles src="Module:Citation/CS1/styles.css"></templatestyles>
- Ketten, Darlene R. (1992). "The Marine Mammal Ear: Specializations for Aquatic Audition and Echolocation". In Webster, Douglas B.; Fay, Richard R.; Popper, Arthur N. *The Evolutionary Biology of Hearing*. Springer–Verlag. pp. 717–750. doi: 10.1007/978-1-4612-2784-7_44[136]. ISBN 978-1-4612-7668-5.<templatestyles src="Module:Citation/CS1/styles.css"></templatestyles>
- Kennedy, Robert; Perrin, W.F.; Wursig, B.; Thewissen, J. G. M. (2008). "Right whales (*E. glacialis, E. japonica*, and *E. australis*"[137]. *Encyclopedia of Marine Mammals*. ISBN 978-0-12-373553-9.<templatestyles src="Module:Citation/CS1/styles.css"></templatestyles>
- Whitehead, H. (2003). *Sperm Whales: Social Evolution in the Ocean*. Chicago: University of Chicago Press. p. 4. ISBN 978-0-226-89518-5.<templatestyles src="Module:Citation/CS1/styles.css"></templatestyles>
- Janet Mann; Richard C. Connor; Peter L. Tyack; et al., eds. (2000). *Cetacean Societies: Field Studies of Dolphins and Whales*[138]. University of Chicago. p. 9. ISBN 0-226-50341-0.<templatestyles src="Module:Citation/CS1/styles.css"></templatestyles>
- Nemoto, T.; Okiyama, M.; Iwasaki, N.; Kikuchi, T. (1988). "Squid as Predators on Krill (Euphausia superba) and Prey for Sperm Whales in the Southern Ocean". In Dietrich Sahrhage. *Antarctic Ocean and Resources*

*Variability*. Springer Berlin Heidelberg. pp. 292–296. doi: 10.1007/978-3-642-73724-4_25[139]. ISBN 978-3-642-73726-8.<templatestyles src="Module:Citation/CS1/styles.css"></templatestyles>
* Riedman, M. (1991). *The Pinnipeds: Seals, Sea Lions, and Walruses*. University of California Press. p. 168. ISBN 0-520-06498-4.<templatestyles src="Module:Citation/CS1/styles.css"></templatestyles>
* Proulx, Jean-Pierre (1994). *Basque whaling in Labrador in the 16th century*. pp. 260–286. ISBN 978-0660148199.<templatestyles src="Module:Citation/CS1/styles.css"></templatestyles>
* Tonnessen, J.N.; Johnsen, A.O (1982). *The History of Modern Whaling*. C. Hurst. ISBN 0-905838-23-8.<templatestyles src="Module:Citation/CS1/styles.css"></templatestyles>
* Mead, J.G.; Brownell, R. L., Jr. (2005). "Order Cetacea". *Mammal Species of the World: A Taxonomic and Geographic Reference*. Johns Hopkins University Press. pp. 723–743. ISBN 978-0-8018-8221-0.<templatestyles src="Module:Citation/CS1/styles.css"></templatestyles>
* Björgvinsson, Ásbjörn; Lugmayr, Helmut; Camm, Martin; Skaptason, Jón (2002). *Whale watching in Iceland*. ISBN 9979-761-55-5.<templatestyles src="Module:Citation/CS1/styles.css"></templatestyles>
* "Lamentations 4:3". *Bible*[140]. Retrieved 29 August 2015.<templatestyles src="Module:Citation/CS1/styles.css"></templatestyles>
* Quran 37:139–148[141]
* "Matthew". *Bible*[142]. Retrieved 30 December 2013.<templatestyles src="Module:Citation/CS1/styles.css"></templatestyles>
* Mack, John (2013). *The Sea: a cultural history*. Reaktion Books. pp. 205–206. ISBN 978-1-78023-184-6.<templatestyles src="Module:Citation/CS1/styles.css"></templatestyles>
* Bonner, Nigel. *Whales*. Facts on File. pp. 17, 23–24. ISBN 0-7137-0887-5.<templatestyles src="Module:Citation/CS1/styles.css"></templatestyles>
* Beland, Pierre (1996). *Beluga: A Farewell to Whales* (1 ed.). The Lyons Press. p. 224. ISBN 1-55821-398-8.<templatestyles src="Module:Citation/CS1/styles.css"></templatestyles>

## Articles

* Gatesy, J. (1997). "More DNA support for a Cetacea/Hippopotamidae clade: the blood-clotting protein gene gamma-fibrinogen"[143] (PDF). *Molecular Biology and Evolution*. **14** (5): 537–543. doi: 10.1093/oxfordjournals.molbev.a025790[144]. PMID 9159931[145].<templatestyles src="Module:Citation/CS1/styles.css"></templatestyles>

- Johnson, James H.; Wolman, Allen A. (1984). "The Humpback Whale". *Marine Fisheries Review*. **46** (4): 30–37.<templatestyles src="Module:Citation/CS1/styles.css"></templatestyles>
- Goldbogen, Jeremy A. (2010). "The Ultimate Mouthful: Lunge Feeding in Rorqual Whales"[146]. *American Scientist*. **98** (2): 124–131. doi: 10.1511/2010.83.124[147].<templatestyles src="Module:Citation/CS1/styles.css"></templatestyles>
- Houben, A. J. P.; Bijl, P. K.; Pross, J.; Bohaty, S. M.; Passchier, S.; Stickley, C. E.; Rohl, U.; Sugisaki, S.; Tauxe, L.; van de Flierdt, T.; Olney, M.; Sangiorgi, F.; Sluijs, A.; Escutia, C.; Brinkhuis, H. (2013). "Reorganization of Southern Ocean Plankton Ecosystem at the Onset of Antarctic Glaciation". *Science*. **340** (6130): 341–344. Bibcode: 2013Sci...340..341H[148]. doi: 10.1126/science.1223646[149]. PMID 23599491[150].<templatestyles src="Module:Citation/CS1/styles.css"></templatestyles>
- Steeman, M. E.; Hebsgaard, M. B.; Fordyce, R. E.; Ho, S. Y. W.; Rabosky, D. L.; Nielsen, R.; Rahbek, C.; Glenner, H.; Sorensen, M. V.; Willerslev, E. (2009). "Radiation of Extant Cetaceans Driven by Restructuring of the Oceans"[151]. *Systematic Biology*. **58** (6): 573–585. doi: 10.1093/sysbio/syp060[152]. PMC 2777972[151]. PMID 20525610[153].<templatestyles src="Module:Citation/CS1/styles.css"></templatestyles>
- Thewissen, J. G. M.; Cooper, L. N.; Clementz, M. T.; Bajpai, S.; Tiwari, B. N. (2007). "Whales originated from aquatic artiodactyls in the Eocene epoch of India"[154] (PDF). *Nature*. **450** (7173): 1190–1194. Bibcode: 2007Natur.450.1190T[155]. doi: 10.1038/nature06343[156]. PMID 18097400[157].<templatestyles src="Module:Citation/CS1/styles.css"></templatestyles>
- Fahlke, Julia M.; Gingerich, Philip D.; Welsh, Robert C.; Wood, Aaron R. (2011). "Cranial asymmetry in Eocene archaeocete whales and the evolution of directional hearing in water"[158]. *Proceedings of the National Academy of Sciences*. **108** (35): 14545–14548. Bibcode: 2011PNAS..10814545F[159]. doi: 10.1073/pnas.1108927108[160]. PMC 3167538[158]. PMID 21873217[161].<templatestyles src="Module:Citation/CS1/styles.css"></templatestyles>
- Bebej, R. M.; ul-Haq, M.; Zalmout, I. S.; Gingerich, P. D. (June 2012). "Morphology and Function of the Vertebral Column in *Remingtonocetus domandaensis* (Mammalia, cetacea) from the Middle Eocene Domanda Formation of Pakistan". *Journal of Mammalian Evolution*. **19** (2): 77–104. doi: 10.1007/S10914-011-9184-8[162].<templatestyles src="Module:Citation/CS1/styles.css"></templatestyles>
- Reidenberg, Joy S. (2007). "Anatomical adaptations of aquatic

mammals"[163]. *The Anatomical Record.* **290** (6): 507–513. doi: 10.1002/ar.20541[164]. PMID 17516440[165].<templatestyles src="Module:Citation/CS1/styles.css"></templatestyles>

- Boisserie, Jean-Renaud; Lihoreau, Fabrice; Brunet, Michel (2005). "The position of Hippopotamidae within Cetartiodactyla"[166]. *Proceedings of the National Academy of Sciences.* **102** (5): 1537–1541. Bibcode: 2005PNAS..102.1537B[167]. doi: 10.1073/pnas.0409518102[168]. PMC 547867[166]. PMID 15677331[169].<templatestyles src="Module:Citation/CS1/styles.css"></templatestyles>
- Scholander, Per Fredrik (1940). "Experimental investigations on the respiratory function in diving mammals and birds". *Hvalraadets Skrifter.* **22**: 1–131.<templatestyles src="Module:Citation/CS1/styles.css"></templatestyles>
- Rose, Kenneth D. (2001). "The Ancestry of Whales"[170] (PDF). *Science.* **293**: 2216–2217. doi: 10.1126/science.1065305[171]. PMID 11567127[172].<templatestyles src="Module:Citation/CS1/styles.css"></templatestyles>
- Norena, S. R.; Williams, T. M. (2000). "Body size and skeletal muscle myoglobin of cetaceans: adaptations for maximizing dive duration". *Comparative Biochemistry and Physiology A.* **126** (2): 181–191. doi: 10.1016/S1095-6433(00)00182-3[173]. PMID 10936758[174].<templatestyles src="Module:Citation/CS1/styles.css"></templatestyles>
- Cranford, T.W.; Krysl, P.; Hildebrand, J.A. (2008). "Acoustic pathways revealed: simulated sound transmission and reception in Cuvier's beaked whale (*Ziphius cavirostris*)". *Bioinspiration & Biomimetics.* **3**: 016001. Bibcode: 2008BiBi....3a6001C[175]. doi: 10.1088/1748-3182/3/1/016001[176]. PMID 18364560[177].<templatestyles src="Module:Citation/CS1/styles.css"></templatestyles>
- Smith, Craig R.; Baco, Amy R. (2003). "Ecology of Whale Falls at the Deep-Sea Floor". *Oceanography and Marine Biology: An Annual Review.* **41**: 311–354.<templatestyles src="Module:Citation/CS1/styles.css"></templatestyles>
- Mass, Alla; Supin, Alexander (21 May 2007). "Adaptive features of aquatic mammals' eyes"[178]. *Anatomical Record.* **290** (6): 701–715. doi: 10.1002/ar.20529[179]. PMID 17516421[180].<templatestyles src="Module:Citation/CS1/styles.css"></templatestyles>
- Watson, K.K.; Jones, T. K.; Allman, J. M. (2006). "Dendritic architecture of the Von Economo neurons". *Neuroscience.* **141** (3): 1107–1112. doi: 10.1016/j.neuroscience.2006.04.084[181]. PMID 16797136[182].<templatestyles src="Module:Citation/CS1/styles.css"></templatestyle

- Hof, Patrick R.; Van Der Gucht, Estel (2007). "Structure of the cerebral cortex of the humpback whale, *Megaptera novaeangliae* (Cetacea, Mysticeti, Balaenopteridae)". *The Anatomical Record*. **290** (1): 1–31. doi: 10.1002/ar.20407[183]. PMID 17441195[184].<templatestyles src="Module:Citation/CS1/styles.css"></templatestyles>
- Wiley, David; et al. (2011). "Underwater components of humpback whale bubble-net feeding behaviour"[185]. *Behaviour*. **148** (5): 575–602. doi: 10.1163/000579511X570893[186].<templatestyles src="Module:Citation/CS1/styles.css"></templatestyles>
- Leighton, Tim; Finfer, Dan; Grover, Ed; White, Paul (2007). "An acoustical hypothesis for the spiral bubble nets of humpback whales, and the implications for whale feeding"[187] (PDF). *Acoustics Bulletin*. **32** (1): 17–21.<templatestyles src="Module:Citation/CS1/styles.css"></templatestyles>
- Zerbini, Alexandre N.; et al. (11 May 2006). "Satellite-monitored movements of humpback whales in the Southwest Atlantic Ocean". *Marine Ecology Progress Series*. **313**: 295–304. Bibcode: 2006MEPS..313..295Z[188]. doi: 10.3354/meps313295[189].<templatestyles src="Module:Citation/CS1/styles.css"></templatestyles>
- Miller, P. J. O.; Aoki, K.; Rendell, L. E.; Amano, M. (2008). "Stereotypical resting behavior of the sperm whale". *Current Biology*. **18** (1): R21–R23. doi: 10.1016/j.cub.2007.11.003[190]. PMID 18177706[191].<templatestyles src="Module:Citation/CS1/styles.css"></templatestyles>
- Lydersen, Christian; Weslawski, Jan Marcin; Øritsland, Nils Are (1991). "Stomach content analysis of minke whales from the Lofoten and Vesterålen areas, Norway"[192]. *Ecography*. **1** (3): 219–222. doi: 10.1111/j.1600-0587.1991.tb00655.x[193].<templatestyles src="Module:Citation/CS1/styles.css"></templatestyles>
- Morrel, Virginia (30 January 2012). "Killer Whale Menu Finally Revealed"[194]. *Science*. Retrieved 29 August 2015.<templatestyles src="Module:Citation/CS1/styles.css"></templatestyles>
- Smith, Thomas G.; Sjare, Becky (1990). "Predation of Belugas and Narwhals by Polar Bears in Nearshore Areas of the Canadian High Arctic". *Arctic*. **43** (2): 99–102. doi: 10.14430/arctic1597[195].<templatestyles src="Module:Citation/CS1/styles.css"></templatestyles>
- Roman, J.; McCarthy, J. J. (October 2010). "The Whale Pump: Marine Mammals Enhance Primary Productivity in a Coastal Basin"[196]. *PLoS ONE*. **5** (10): e13255. Bibcode: 2010PLoSO...513255R[197]. doi: 10.1371/journal.pone.0013255[198]. PMC 2952594[196]. PMID 20949007[199].<templatestyles src="Module:Citation/CS1/styles.css"></templatestyles>

- Roman, J.; McCarthy, J. J. (2010). Roopnarine, Peter, ed. "The Whale Pump: Marine Mammals Enhance Primary Productivity in a Coastal Basin"[200]. *PLoS ONE*. **5** (10): e13255. Bibcode: 2010PLoSO...513255R[197]. doi: 10.1371/journal.pone.0013255[198]. PMC 2952594[196]. PMID 20949007[199].<templatestyles src="Module:Citation/CS1/styles.css"></templatestyles>
- Roman, Joe; Estes, James A.; Morissette, Lyne; Smith, Craig; Costa, Daniel; McCarthy, James; Nation, J.B.; Nicol, Stephen; Pershing, Andrew; Smetacek, Victor (2014). "Whales as marine ecosystem engineers". *Frontiers in Ecology and the Environment*. **12** (7): 377–385. doi: 10.1890/130220[201].<templatestyles src="Module:Citation/CS1/styles.css"></templatestyles>
- Nummela, Sirpa; Thewissen, J.G.M; Bajpai, Sunil; Hussain, Taseer; Kumar, Kishor (2007). "Sound transmission in archaic and modern whales: Anatomical adaptations for underwater hearing". *The Anatomical Record*. **290** (6): 716–733. doi: 10.1002/ar.20528[202]. PMID 17516434[203].<templatestyles src="Module:Citation/CS1/styles.css"></templatestyles>
- Fujiwara, Yoshihiro; et al. (16 February 2007). "Three-year investigations into sperm whale-fall ecosystems in Japan". *Marine Ecology*. **28** (1): 219–230. Bibcode: 2007MarEc..28..219F[204]. doi: 10.1111/j.1439-0485.2007.00150.x[205].<templatestyles src="Module:Citation/CS1/styles.css"></templatestyles>
- Morseth, C. Michele (1997). "Twentieth-Century Changes in Beluga Whale Hunting and Butchering by the Kaŋiġmiut of Buckland, Alaska". *Arctic*. **50** (3): 241. doi: 10.14430/arctic1106[206]. JSTOR 40511703[207].<templatestyles src="Module:Citation/CS1/styles.css"></templatestyles>
- Rommel, S. A.; et al. (2006). "Elements of beaked whale anatomy and diving physiology and some hypothetical causes of sonar-related stranding". *Journal of Cetacean Resource Management*. **7** (3): 189–209.<templatestyles src="Module:Citation/CS1/styles.css"></templatestyles>
- Schrope, Mark. (2003). "Whale deaths caused by US Navy's sonar". *Nature*. **415** (6868): 106. Bibcode: 2002Natur.415..106S[208]. doi: 10.1038/415106a[209]. PMID 11805797[210].<templatestyles src="Module:Citation/CS1/styles.css"></templatestyles>
- Piantadosi, C. A.; Thalmann, E. D. (2004). "Pathology: whales, sonar and decompression sickness". *Nature*. **428** (6894): 716–718. doi: 10.1038/nature02527a[211]. PMID 15085881[212].<templatestyles src="Module:Citation/CS1/styles.css"></templatestyles>
- "North Atlantic Right Whale Source Document for the Critical Habitat Designation: A review of information pertaining to the definition

of "critical habitat"". NOAA Fisheries. July 2014.<templatestyles src="Module:Citation/CS1/styles.css"></templatestyles>

- Laidre, K. L.; Stirling, I.; Lowry, L. F.; Wiig, Ø.; Heide-Jørgensen, M. P.; Ferguson, S.H. (2008). "Quantifying the sensitivity of Arctic marine mammals to climate-induced habitat change"[213] (PDF). *Ecological Applications*. **18** (2 Suppl.): S97–S125. doi: 10.1890/06-0546.1[214]. PMID 18494365[215]. Archived from the original[216] (PDF) on 24 September 2015. Retrieved 29 August 2015.<templatestyles src="Module:Citation/CS1/styles.css"></templatestyles>

- Cressey, Jason (1998). "Making a Splash in the Pacific Ocean: Dolphin and Whale Myths and Legends of Oceania"[217] (PDF). *Rapa Nui Journal*. **12**: 75–84. Retrieved 5 August 2015.<templatestyles src="Module:Citation/CS1/styles.css"></templatestyles>

## Websites

- Froias, Gustin (2012). "Balaenidae"[218]. New Bedford Whaling Museum. Retrieved 29 August 2015.<templatestyles src="Module:Citation/CS1/styles.css"></templatestyles>

- Jefferson, T.A.; Leatherwood, S.; Webber, M.A. "Gray whale (Family Eschrichtiidae)"[219]. Marine Species Identification Portal. Retrieved 29 August 2015.<templatestyles src="Module:Citation/CS1/styles.css"></templatestyles>

- Jefferson, T.A.; Leatherwood, S.; Webber, M.A. "Narwhal and White Whale (Family Monodontidae)"[220]. Marine Species Identification Portal. Retrieved 29 August 2015.<templatestyles src="Module:Citation/CS1/styles.css"></templatestyles>

- Jefferson, T.A.; Leatherwood, S.; Webber, M.A. "Sperm Whale (Family Physeteridae)"[221]. Marine Species Identification Portal. Retrieved 29 August 2015.<templatestyles src="Module:Citation/CS1/styles.css"></templatestyles>

- Jefferson, T.A.; Leatherwood, S.; Webber, M.A. "Beaked Whales (Family Ziphiidae)"[222]. Marine Species Identification Portal. Retrieved 29 August 2015.<templatestyles src="Module:Citation/CS1/styles.css"></templatestyles>

- "Going Aquatic: Cetacean Evolution"[223]. PBS Nature. 21 March 2012. Retrieved 29 August 2015.<templatestyles src="Module:Citation/CS1/styles.css"></templatestyles>

- Interglot translation dictionary. "Ballena asesina"[224]. *interglot.com*. Retrieved 15 January 2016.<templatestyles src="Module:Citation/CS1/styles.css"></templatestyles>

- "Introduction to Cetacea: Archaeocetes: The Oldest Whales"[225]. University of Berkeley. Retrieved 25 July 2015.<templatestyles src="Module:Citation/CS1/styles.css"></templatestyles>
- "Sperm Whales brain size"[226]. NOAA Fisheries – Office of Protected Resources. Retrieved 9 August 2015.<templatestyles src="Module:Citation/CS1/styles.css"></templatestyles>
- "Mysticetes hunt in groups"[227]. Defenders of Wildlife. Retrieved July 24, 2015.<templatestyles src="Module:Citation/CS1/styles.css"></templatestyles>
- Marrero, Meghan E.; Thornton, Stuart (1 November 2011). "Big Fish: A Brief History of Whaling"[228]. National Geographic. Retrieved 2 September 2015.<templatestyles src="Module:Citation/CS1/styles.css"></templatestyles>
- "Whale products"[229]. New Bedford Whaling Museum. Retrieved 29 August 2015.<templatestyles src="Module:Citation/CS1/styles.css"></templatestyles>
- Stonehouse, Bernard (5 October 2007). "British Arctic whaling: an overview"[230]. University of Hull. Retrieved 4 September 2015.<templatestyles src="Module:Citation/CS1/styles.css"></templatestyles>
- "Timeline: The History of Whaling in America"[231]. PBS.<templatestyles src="Module:Citation/CS1/styles.css"></templatestyles>
- "Which countries are still whaling"[232]. International Fund for Animal Welfare. Retrieved 29 August 2015.<templatestyles src="Module:Citation/CS1/styles.css"></templatestyles>
- "Aboriginal Subsistence whaling"[233]. IWC. Retrieved 29 August 2015.<templatestyles src="Module:Citation/CS1/styles.css"></templatestyles>
- NOAA Fisheries – Office of Protected Resources. "The Tuna-Dolphin Issue"[234]. *noaa.gov*. Retrieved 29 August 2015.<templatestyles src="Module:Citation/CS1/styles.css"></templatestyles>
- "The physics of bubble rings and other diver's exhausts"[235]. Archived from the original[236] on 6 October 2006. Retrieved 19 December 2015.<templatestyles src="Module:Citation/CS1/styles.css"></templatestyles>
- Metcalfe, C. (23 February 2012). "Persistent organic pollutants in the marine food chain"[237]. United Nations University. Retrieved 16 August 2013.<templatestyles src="Module:Citation/CS1/styles.css"></templatestyles>
- unknown. "Key Documents"[238]. *International Whaling Commission*. Retrieved 29 August 2015.<templatestyles src="Module:Citation/CS1/styles.css"></templatestyles>

- "Catch limits"[239]. *International Whaling Commission.* Retrieved 6 August 2015.<templatestyles src="Module:Citation/CS1/styles.css"></templatestyles>
- MacKenzie, Debora (4 June 1994). "Whales win southern sanctuary"[240]. New Scientist. Retrieved 12 September 2015.<templatestyles src="Module:Citation/CS1/styles.css"></templatestyles>
- "Whale Sanctuaries"[241]. International Whaling Commission. Retrieved 4 September 2015.<templatestyles src="Module:Citation/CS1/styles.css"></templatestyles>
- O'Connor, Simon (2009). "Whale Watching Worldwide"[242] (PDF). International Fund for Animal Welfare. pp. 23–24. Retrieved 26 December 2014.<templatestyles src="Module:Citation/CS1/styles.css"></templatestyles>
- National Oceanic and Atmospheric Administration, NOAA (January 2004). "Marine Wildlife Viewing Guidelines"[243] (PDF). Retrieved 6 August 2010.<templatestyles src="Module:Citation/CS1/styles.css"></templatestyles>
- O'Connor S.; Campbell R.; Cortez H.; Knowles T. (2009). "Whale Watching Worldwide: tourism numbers, expenditures and expanding economic benefits"[242] (PDF). *International Fund for Animal Welfare.* Retrieved 29 August 2015.<templatestyles src="Module:Citation/CS1/styles.css"></templatestyles>
- Viegas, Jennifer (23 February 2010). "Thousands Mourn Dead Whale in Vietnam"[244]. *Discovery News.* Retrieved 15 April 2011.<templatestyles src="Module:Citation/CS1/styles.css"></templatestyles>
- "Funeral for a Whale held at Apam"[245]. *Ghana News Agency.* GhanaWeb. 10 August 2005. Retrieved 15 April 2011.<templatestyles src="Module:Citation/CS1/styles.css"></templatestyles>
- Hovhannes, Alan (1970). "And God Created Great Whales"[246]. Retrieved 10 October 2007.<templatestyles src="Module:Citation/CS1/styles.css"></templatestyles>
- "Beluga Whales in Captivity: Hunted, Poisoned, Unprotected". *Special Report on Captivity 2006.* Canadian Marine Environment Protection Society. 2006. Missing or empty |url= (help); |access-date= requires |url= (help)<templatestyles src="Module:Citation/CS1/styles.css"></templatestyles>
- "Beluga (*Delphinapterus leucas*) Facts – Distribution – In the Zoo"[247]. World Association of Zoos and Aquariums. Retrieved 5 December 2011.<templatestyles src="Module:Citation/CS1/styles.css"></templatestyles>
- "The Story of Navy Dolphins"[248]. PBS. Retrieved 12 October 2008.<templatestyles

src="Module:Citation/CS1/styles.css"></templatestyles>

## News

- Northeastern Ohio Universities Colleges of Medicine and Pharmacy (2007). "Whales Descended From Tiny Deer-like Ancestors"[249]. Retrieved 21 December 2007.<templatestyles src="Module:Citation/CS1/styles.css"></templatestyles>
- "New Dawn". *Walking with Prehistoric Beasts*. 2002. Discovery Channel. |access-date= requires |url= (help)<templatestyles src="Module:Citation/CS1/styles.css"></templatestyles>
- Collins, Nick (22 October 2012). "Whale learns to mimic human speech"[250]. Retrieved 22 October 2012.<templatestyles src="Module:Citation/CS1/styles.css"></templatestyles>
- Siebert, Charles (8 July 2009). "Watching Whales Watching Us"[251]. *New York Times Magazine*. Retrieved 29 August 2015.<templatestyles src="Module:Citation/CS1/styles.css"></templatestyles>
- Fields, R. Douglas. "Are whales smarter than we are?"[252]. Retrieved 9 August 2015.<templatestyles src="Module:Citation/CS1/styles.css"></templatestyles>
- Griffin, Catherine (7 December 2015). "Beluga Bubbles Reveal How These Whales Are Feeling"[253]. Retrieved 19 December 2015.<templatestyles src="Module:Citation/CS1/styles.css"></templatestyles>
- "Milk". *Modern Marvels*. Season 14. 2008-01-07. The History Channel. |access-date= requires |url= (help)<templatestyles src="Module:Citation/CS1/styles.css"></templatestyles>
- "Whale poop pumps up ocean health"[254]. 12 October 2010. Retrieved 18 November 2011.<templatestyles src="Module:Citation/CS1/styles.css"></templatestyles>
- "Whale poo important for ocean ecosystems"[255]. *Australian Geographic*. 26 May 2014. Retrieved 18 November 2014.<templatestyles src="Module:Citation/CS1/styles.css"></templatestyles>
- "Rock art hints at whaling origins"[256]. 20 April 2004. Retrieved 2 September 2015. <q>Stone Age people may have started hunting whales as early as 6,000 BC, new evidence from South Korea suggests.</q><templatestyles src="Module:Citation/CS1/styles.css"></templatestyles>
- "Commercial Whaling: Good Whale Hunting"[257]. *The Economist*. 4 March 2012. Retrieved 1 September 2015.<templatestyles src="Module:Citation/CS1/styles.css"></templatestyles>
- Ford, Catherine (July 2015). "A Savage History: Whaling in the South Pacific and Southern Oceans"[258]. *The Monthly:*

*Australian politics, societies, and cultures.*<templatestyles src="Module:Citation/CS1/styles.css"></templatestyles>

- Tsai, Wen-Chu. "Whales and trash-bags"[259]. *Taipei Times*. Retrieved 5 August 2015.<templatestyles src="Module:Citation/CS1/styles.css"></templatestyles>

- Kirby, Alex (8 October 2003). "Sonar may cause Whale deaths"[260]. Retrieved 14 September 2006.<templatestyles src="Module:Citation/CS1/styles.css"></templatestyles>

- "CWA travels to The Petroglyphs of Bangudae"[261]. *Current World Archaeology*. 24 January 2014. Retrieved 31 August 2015.<templatestyles src="Module:Citation/CS1/styles.css"></templatestyles>

- "Thousand gather for whale's funeral in Vietnam"[262]. *The Independent*. Associated Press. 23 February 2010. Retrieved 15 April 2011.<templatestyles src="Module:Citation/CS1/styles.css"></templatestyles>

- "Whale funeral draws 1000 mourners in Vietnam"[263]. *Sydney Morning Herald*. AFP. 14 April 2003. Retrieved 15 April 2011.<templatestyles src="Module:Citation/CS1/styles.css"></templatestyles>

# Further reading

- O'Connell, M.; Berrow, S. (2015). "Records from the Irish Whales and Dolphin Group for 2013". *Irish Naturalists' Journal*. **34** (2): 154–161.<templatestyles src="Module:Citation/CS1/styles.css"></templatestyles>

- ⊚ "Whale". *New International Encyclopedia*. 1905.<templatestyles src="Module:Citation/CS1/styles.css"></templatestyles>

# Appendix

## References

[1]//en.wikipedia.org/w/index.php?title=Whale&action=edit
[2]Skeat 1898.
[3]Leatherwood et al. 1991, pp. 33–65.
[4]Klinowska et al. 1991a, p. 4.
[5]Gatesy 1997.
[6]Johnson et al. 1984, *Megaptera novaeangliae* http://spo.nwr.noaa.gov/mfr464/mfr4647.pdf.
[7]Cozzi et al. 2009.
[8]Goldbogen 2010.
[9]Froias 2012.
[10]Jefferson et al.
[11]Jeanette et al. 1990, pp. 203–427.
[12]Jefferson 2015a.
[13]Jefferson 2015b.
[14]Jefferson 2015c.
[15]ScienceDaily 2007.
[16]Dawkins 2004.
[17]Berkeley.
[18]Thewissen 2007.
[19]Falkhe et al. 2011.
[20]Kenneth 2001.
[21]Bebej et al. 2012.
[22]Reidenberg 2012, p. 508.
[23]Boisserie et al. 2005, pp. 1537–1541.
[24]PBSa 2012.
[25]Houben et al. 2013, pp. 341–344.
[26]Steeman et al. 2009, pp. 573–585.
[27]Reidenberg 2012, pp. 510–511.
[28]Ralls 1984, pp. 1005–1011.
[29]Reidenberg 2012, pp. 509–510.
[30]Reidenberg 2012, pp. 507–508.
[31]Scholander 1940.
[32]Klinowska et al. 1991a, p. 5.
[33]Reidenberg 2012, p. 510.
[34]Edward 1995, p. 11.
[35]Klinowska et al. 1991a, p. 122–262.
[36]Reidenberg 2012, pp. 508.
[37]Norena et al. 2000, pp. 181–191.
[38]Cranford et al. 2008.
[39]Nummela 2007, pp. 716–733.
[40]Jeanette et al. 1990, pp. 1–19.
[41]Reidenberg 2012, p. 512.
[42]Thewissen 2002.
[43]Ketten 1992, pp. 717–750.
[44]Mass et al. 2007, pp. 701–715.
[45]Jeanette et al. 1990, pp. 505–519.
[46]Reidenberg 2012, pp. 512.
[47]Jeanette et al. 1990, pp. 481–505.
[48]Jeanette et al. 1990, pp. 447–455.
[49]Whitehead 2003, p. 4.
[50]Collins 2012.

[51] Mann 2000, p. 9.
[52] Siebert 2009.
[53] Watson 2006, pp. 1107–1112.
[54] Hof 2007, pp. 1–31.
[55] NOAAa.
[56] Fields.
[57] Metcalfe.
[58] Griffin 2015.
[59] Wiley 2011, pp. 575–602.
[60] Leighton et al. 2007, pp. 17–21.
[61] Modern Marvels 2007.
[62] Johnson et al., *Megaptera novaeangliae* http://spo.nwr.noaa.gov/mfr464/mfr4647.pdf.
[63] Zerbini 2006, *Megaptera novaeanglia* http://faculty.washington.edu/glennvb/fish475/Zerbini%
20et%20al%202006%20published%20paper.pdf pp. 295–304.
[64] Kennedy 2008, p. 966.
[65] Miller et al. 2008, pp. 21–23.
[66] Nemoto et al. 1988, pp. 292–296.
[67] Lydersen et al. 1991, *Balaenoptera acutorostrata* http://onlinelibrary.wiley.com/doi/10.1111/j.
1600-0587.1991.tb00655.x/abstract.
[68] Defenders of Wildlife.
[69] Klinowska et al. 1991a, p. 122–162.
[70] Riedman 1991, p. 168.
[71] Morrel 2012.
[72] Smith et al. 1990, *Delphinapterus leucus* http://pubs.aina.ucalgary.ca/arctic/Arctic43-2-99.pdf
pp. 99–102.
[73] Roman 2010a, The Whale Pump http://www.plosone.org/article/info%3Adoi%2F10.1371%
2Fjournal.pone.0013255.
[74] ScienceDaily 2010.
[75] Roman 2010b.
[76] Geographic 2014.
[77] Roman et al. 2014.
[78] Smith et al. 2003, The Whale Fall http://www.soest.hawaii.edu/oceanography/faculty/csmith/
Files/Smith%20and%20Baco%202003.pdf pp. 311–354.
[79] Fujiwara 2007, The Whale Fall http://onlinelibrary.wiley.com/doi/10.1111/j.1439-0485.2007.
00150.x/pdf pp. 219–230.
[80] BBC 2004.
[81] Morrero 2011.
[82] Ford 2015.
[83] Proulx 1994, pp. 260–286.
[84] New Bedford.
[85] Stonehouse 2007.
[86] Tonnessen 1982.
[87] PBS.
[88] Economist 2012.
[89] IFAW.
[90] Klinowska et al. 1991a, p. 13.
[91] IWCa.
[92] Morseth 1997.
[93] NOAAb.
[94] Metcalfe 2012.
[95] Tsai.
[96] References prior to 2010, before a more definitive conclusion:
[97] IWCb.
[98] IWCc, Catches taken https://iwc.int/catches#comm.
[99] NOAAc, *Eubalaena glacialis* http://www.greateratlantic.fisheries.noaa.gov/regs/2015/
February/narwsourcedocumentfinal072114.pdf.

[100] MacKenzie 1994.
[101] IWCd.
[102] Mead 2005, pp. 723–743.
[103] Laidre 2008, pp. 97–125.
[104] IFAW 2009.
[105] NOAA 2004.
[106] Björgvinsson 2002.
[107] O'Connor 2009.
[108] CWA 2014.
[109] Cressey 1998.
[110] The Independent 2010.
[111] AFP 2003.
[112] Viegas 2010.
[113] GNA 2005.
[114] Lamentations.
[115] Quran.
[116] Matthew.
[117] Mack 2013.
[118] Hovhannes 1970.
[119] NYT 1861.
[120] CMEPS 2006.
[121] WAZA.
[122] Bonner.
[123] PBSb.
[124] Beland 1996.
[125] Klinowska et al. 1991a, p. 279.
[126] Klinowska et al. 1991a, pp. 372–373.
[127] Klinowska et al. 1991a, p. 383.
[128] Klinowska et al. 1991a, p. 421.
[129] https://portals.iucn.org/library/sites/library/files/documents/RD-1991-001.pdf
[130] https://books.google.com/books?id=VWz1BwAAQBAJ&pg=PA1
[131] //doi.org/10.1007%2F978-1-4899-0858-2
[132] //www.amazon.com/dp/B00KX9I8Y8
[133] https://books.google.com/books?id=vDZAAAAAYAAJ&pg=PA704
[134] http://www.cetus.ucsd.edu/SIO133/PDF/Sexual%20Dimorphism.pdf
[135] https://books.google.com/books?id=DZuAsci2apAC&pg=PA11
[136] //doi.org/10.1007%2F978-1-4612-2784-7_44
[137] https://books.google.com/books?id=2rkHQpToi9sC&pg=PA966
[138] https://books.google.com/books?id=W-UQNoxMONwC
[139] //doi.org/10.1007%2F978-3-642-73724-4_25
[140] http://biblehub.com/lamentations/4-3.htm
[141] http://www.perseus.tufts.edu/hopper/text?doc=Perseus%3Atext%3A2002.02.0006%3Asura%3D37%3Averse%3D139
[142] https://www.biblegateway.com/passage/?search=jonah+1-4
[143] http://mbe.oxfordjournals.org/content/14/5/537.full.pdf
[144] //doi.org/10.1093%2Foxfordjournals.molbev.a025790
[145] //www.ncbi.nlm.nih.gov/pubmed/9159931
[146] http://www.americanscientist.org/issues/pub/the-ultimate-mouthful-lunge-feeding-in-rorqual-whales
[147] //doi.org/10.1511%2F2010.83.124
[148] http://adsabs.harvard.edu/abs/2013Sci...340..341H
[149] //doi.org/10.1126%2Fscience.1223646
[150] //www.ncbi.nlm.nih.gov/pubmed/23599491
[151] //www.ncbi.nlm.nih.gov/pmc/articles/PMC2777972
[152] //doi.org/10.1093%2Fsysbio%2Fsyp060
[153] //www.ncbi.nlm.nih.gov/pubmed/20525610

[154]http://repository.ias.ac.in/4642/1/316.pdf
[155]http://adsabs.harvard.edu/abs/2007Natur.450.1190T
[156]//doi.org/10.1038%2Fnature06343
[157]//www.ncbi.nlm.nih.gov/pubmed/18097400
[158]//www.ncbi.nlm.nih.gov/pmc/articles/PMC3167538
[159]http://adsabs.harvard.edu/abs/2011PNAS..10814545F
[160]//doi.org/10.1073%2Fpnas.1108927108
[161]//www.ncbi.nlm.nih.gov/pubmed/21873217
[162]//doi.org/10.1007%2FS10914-011-9184-8
[163]http://onlinelibrary.wiley.com/doi/10.1002/ar.20541/pdf
[164]//doi.org/10.1002%2Far.20541
[165]//www.ncbi.nlm.nih.gov/pubmed/17516440
[166]//www.ncbi.nlm.nih.gov/pmc/articles/PMC547867
[167]http://adsabs.harvard.edu/abs/2005PNAS..102.1537B
[168]//doi.org/10.1073%2Fpnas.0409518102
[169]//www.ncbi.nlm.nih.gov/pubmed/15677331
[170]http://courses.washington.edu/biol354/Rose_Science_WHIPPO.pdf
[171]//doi.org/10.1126%2Fscience.1065305
[172]//www.ncbi.nlm.nih.gov/pubmed/11567127
[173]//doi.org/10.1016%2FS1095-6433%2800%2900182-3
[174]//www.ncbi.nlm.nih.gov/pubmed/10936758
[175]http://adsabs.harvard.edu/abs/2008BiBi....3a6001C
[176]//doi.org/10.1088%2F1748-3182%2F3%2F1%2F016001
[177]//www.ncbi.nlm.nih.gov/pubmed/18364560
[178]http://onlinelibrary.wiley.com/doi/10.1002/ar.20529/full
[179]//doi.org/10.1002%2Far.20529
[180]//www.ncbi.nlm.nih.gov/pubmed/17516421
[181]//doi.org/10.1016%2Fj.neuroscience.2006.04.084
[182]//www.ncbi.nlm.nih.gov/pubmed/16797136
[183]//doi.org/10.1002%2Far.20407
[184]//www.ncbi.nlm.nih.gov/pubmed/17441195
[185]http://booksandjournals.brillonline.com/content/journals/10.1163/000579511x570893
[186]//doi.org/10.1163%2F000579511X570893
[187]http://eprints.soton.ac.uk/45654/1/Spiral_net__Leighton__web_1.pdf
[188]http://adsabs.harvard.edu/abs/2006MEPS..313..295Z
[189]//doi.org/10.3354%2Fmeps313295
[190]//doi.org/10.1016%2Fj.cub.2007.11.003
[191]//www.ncbi.nlm.nih.gov/pubmed/18177706
[192]http://onlinelibrary.wiley.com/doi/10.1111/j.1600-0587.1991.tb00655.x/abstract
[193]//doi.org/10.1111%2Fj.1600-0587.1991.tb00655.x
[194]http://news.sciencemag.org/plants-animals/2012/01/killer-whale-menu-finally-revealed
[195]//doi.org/10.14430%2Farctic1597
[196]//www.ncbi.nlm.nih.gov/pmc/articles/PMC2952594
[197]http://adsabs.harvard.edu/abs/2010PLoSO...513255R
[198]//doi.org/10.1371%2Fjournal.pone.0013255
[199]//www.ncbi.nlm.nih.gov/pubmed/20949007
[200]http://journals.plos.org/plosone/article?id=10.1371/journal.pone.0013255
[201]//doi.org/10.1890%2F130220
[202]//doi.org/10.1002%2Far.20528
[203]//www.ncbi.nlm.nih.gov/pubmed/17516434
[204]http://adsabs.harvard.edu/abs/2007MarEc..28..219F
[205]//doi.org/10.1111%2Fj.1439-0485.2007.00150.x
[206]//doi.org/10.14430%2Farctic1106
[207]//www.jstor.org/stable/40511703
[208]http://adsabs.harvard.edu/abs/2002Natur.415..106S
[209]//doi.org/10.1038%2F415106a

[210] //www.ncbi.nlm.nih.gov/pubmed/11805797
[211] //doi.org/10.1038%2Fnature02527a
[212] //www.ncbi.nlm.nih.gov/pubmed/15085881
[213] https://web.archive.org/web/20150924075420/http://www.polarbearsinternational.org/sites/default/files/laidre_et_al._arctic_marmam_and_climate_2008.pdf
[214] //doi.org/10.1890%2F06-0546.1
[215] //www.ncbi.nlm.nih.gov/pubmed/18494365
[216] http://www.polarbearsinternational.org/sites/default/files/laidre_et_al._arctic_marmam_and_climate_2008.pdf
[217] http://islandheritage.org/wordpress/wp-content/uploads/2010/06/RNJ_12_3_Cressey.pdf
[218] http://www.whalingmuseum.org/learn/about-cetaceans/Balaenidae
[219] http://species-identification.org/species.php?species_group=marine_mammals&id=15&menuentry=groepen
[220] http://species-identification.org/species.php?species_group=marine_mammals&id=21&menuentry=groepen
[221] http://species-identification.org/species.php?species_group=marine_mammals&id=23&menuentry=groepen
[222] http://species-identification.org/species.php?species_group=marine_mammals&id=26&menuentry=groepen
[223] https://www.pbs.org/wnet/nature/ocean-giants-going-aquatic-cetacean-evolution/7577/
[224] http://www.interglot.com/dictionary/es/en/search?q=ballena%20asesina
[225] http://www.ucmp.berkeley.edu/mammal/cetacea/cetacean.html
[226] http://www.nmfs.noaa.gov/pr/species/mammals/cetaceans/spermwhale.htm
[227] http://www.defenders.org/whales/basic-facts
[228] http://education.nationalgeographic.com/news/big-fish-history-whaling/
[229] http://www.whalingmuseum.org/learn/research-topics/overview-of-north-american-whaling/whales-hunting
[230] http://www.hull.ac.uk/baw/overview/overview.htm
[231] https://www.pbs.org/wgbh/americanexperience/features/timeline/timeline-whaling/
[232] http://www.ifaw.org/united-states/our-work/whales/which-countries-are-still-whaling
[233] https://iwc.int/aboriginal
[234] http://swfsc.noaa.gov/textblock.aspx?Division=PRD&ParentMenuId=228&id=1408
[235] https://web.archive.org/web/20061006163548/http://www.deepocean.net/deepocean/index.php?science09.php
[236] http://www.deepocean.net/deepocean/index.php?science09.php
[237] http://unu.edu/publications/articles/persistent-organic-pollutants-in-the-marine-food-chain.html
[238] https://iwc.int/convention
[239] https://iwc.int/catches
[240] https://www.newscientist.com/article/mg14219280-900-whales-win-southern-sanctuary/
[241] https://iwc.int/sanctuaries
[242] http://www.ifaw.org/sites/default/files/whale_watching_worldwide.pdf
[243] http://www.nmfs.noaa.gov/pr/pdfs/education/viewing_wildlife.pdf
[244] http://news.discovery.com/animals/thousands-mourn-dead-whale-in-vietnam.html
[245] http://www.ghanaweb.com/GhanaHomePage/NewsArchive/artikel.php?ID=87737
[246] http://www.artistdirect.com/nad/store/artist/album/0,,197507,00.html
[247] http://www.waza.org/en/zoo/visit-the-zoo/aquatic-mammals-1254385523/delphinapterus-leucas
[248] https://www.pbs.org/wgbh/pages/frontline/shows/whales/etc/navycron.html
[249] https://www.sciencedaily.com/releases/2007/12/071220220241.htm
[250] https://www.telegraph.co.uk/news/science/science-news/9625687/Whale-learns-to-mimic-human-speech.html
[251] https://www.nytimes.com/2009/07/12/magazine/12whales-t.html?pagewanted=all
[252] http://blogs.scientificamerican.com/news-blog/are-whales-smarter-than-we-are/
[253] http://www.scienceworldreport.com/articles/34203/20151207/beluga-bubbles-reveal-whales-feeling.htm

[254] https://www.sciencedaily.com/releases/2010/10/101012101255.htm

[255] http://www.australiangeographic.com.au/news/2014/05/whale-poo-important-for-ocean-ecosystems

[256] http://news.bbc.co.uk/1/hi/sci/tech/3638853.stm

[257] https://www.economist.com/blogs/babbage/2012/03/commercial-whaling

[258] https://www.themonthly.com.au/issue/2013/july/1372600800/catherine-ford/savage-history-whaling-pacific-and-southern-oceans

[259] http://www.taipeitimes.com/News/taiwan/archives/2015/07/03/2003622174

[260] http://news.bbc.co.uk/2/hi/science/nature/3173942.stm

[261] http://www.world-archaeology.com/travel/cwa-travels-to-the-petroglyphs-of-bangudae.htm

[262] https://www.independent.co.uk/news/world/asia/thousand-gather-for-whales-funeral-in-vietnam-1907716.html

[263] http://www.smh.com.au/articles/2003/04/13/1050172476288.html

# Article Sources and Contributors

The sources listed for each article provide more detailed licensing information including the copyright status, the copyright owner, and the license conditions.

**Whale**  *Source:*  https://en.wikipedia.org/w/index.php?oldid=859709183  *License:*  Creative Commons Attribution-Share Alike 3.0 *Contributors:*  93, Aa77zz, Abyssal, Acaeton, Acopyeditor, Ankit2299, Anmcelroy, Axl, Bender235, Bgwhite, Blanche of King's Lynn, Bloodofox, Bri, Bubblesorg, Bueller 007, Burklemore1, Cheeseman Muncher, Chiswick Chap, Chris the speller, ClueBot NG, CommonsDelinker, Cygnis insignis, DMacks, Darorcilmir, Dcirovic, Dger, Drmies, Dunkleosteus77, Egsan Bacon, Elmidae, ErikHaugen, Fieryjaguar1, Fnorp, Folklorebuff, Frietjes, Georgia guy, Girth Summit, Graham87, GünniX, Hardin015, Headbomb, Hijiri88, IVORK, Ira Leviton, JeR, Jjfredregill, JoeSperrazza, John, Jon Kolbert, Jonesey95, Jytdog, JzG, Kim9988, Kozan Huseyin, Krakkos, Kudpung, Kuru, LadymooN, Leptictidium, Lfstevens, Library Guy, LittleJerry, LjL, Loraof, Mad Bunny, Mandruss, Maunus, Mountaincirque, Mr Stephen, MrAwesome888, Narky Blert, Neozoen, Nergaal, Niceguyedc, Nihiltres, Nurg, Odeleongt, Osborne, Pbsouth-wood, Pkbwcgs, Plagktos, Plantdrew, Punetor i Rregullt5, R'n'B, Rcsprinter123, Rex123456058, Rhinopias, Richerman, Rjwilmsi, Rtkat3, SophieWhitton, Spicemix, Srednuas Lenoroc, StarryGrandma, Student7, Tim riley, Tom.Reding, WOSlinker, Watisfictie, Zppix  ...................................1

# Image Sources, Licenses and Contributors

The sources listed for each image provide more detailed licensing information including the copyright status, the copyright owner, and the license conditions.

# License

# Index